This book was read first by:

....

Other Murray the Milkman Stories

MURRAY MEETS TIP TOP VILLAGE

FLOWERS & SEEDS

ISBN 978-0-9556068-2-3

Published by Icon Learning
© 2008 Icon Learning Ltd
Text copyright © 2008 Icon Learning Ltd
Illustrations copyright © 2008 Icon Learning Ltd

Additional Artwork provided by Mollie Balogun & Stephen Molokwu

Please visit our website: www.readaware.com

Icon Learning Ltd, PO Box 61407,
Willesden, London, NW10 4US, UK

Murray The Milkman

The Baker's cakes that couldn't be late!

By

Stephen Molokwu

One sunny day Murray was driving down Tip Top High Street in the Milk-mobile, listening to his tunes.

"My last delivery this morning is for Bernard the Baker," he said.

Murray had arrived at the Bakery. He went to the back of the milk-mobile and got out 4 bottles of silver top.

"Bernard sure likes full fat milk. That's a little unhealthy," smiled Murray.

When Murray entered the bakery he saw that Bernard was very upset.

"Oh Murray!" cried Bernard. "My orders are late. I have not delivered my bread to the schools, my rolls to the Royces, my baps to the Browns, or my cakes to the Carters!"

"Take a breath man," said Murray. "Maybe I can help you. What if I deliver some of your orders?"

Bernard smiled. "Really?" he asked.

"Yes," replied Murray.

Bernard shook Murray's hand. "So kind. Thank you very much," said Bernard.

Murray had left Bernard's bakery and was driving in the milk-mobile on his way to deliver some bread.

"That Bernard is funny," smiled Murray. "I think all that baking goes to his head sometimes." He stopped outside the school.

Miss Twitch came to the school gate with Dionne and Daniel. "Hi Uncle Murray!" they shouted.

"Hello Murray" smiled Miss Twitch

Murray was holding a tray of circle shaped bread. "I've got the school bread," he said.

Daniel looked at the bread on the tray. "Hey Miss Twitch, they've got holes in them," he said. "They look a bit like doughnuts."

"Yes they do actually, but they're called Bagels," said Miss Twitch.

Dionne stuck her tongue out at Daniel. "The only doughnut round here is you," she said to him.

Murray and Miss Twitch frowned at her.

"That's enough of that I think," said Miss Twitch.

In the distance, Rascal was hiding behind a post box.

"You can keep the bread," said Rascal to himself. "I just want that tasty milk. Tasty, miow!"

Murray pulled out another tray of bread. The bread was shaped a little bit like a banana. "Do you know what these are called Dionne?" he asked.

"I've seen those before," she replied. "Mum eats those in the morning. They're called croissants."

Miss Twitch smiled. "That's right, very good Dionne," she said.

"Uncle Murray, Uncle Murray!" Daniel shouted. "Dad likes 'Hard-dough' bread."

"I like it too," said Murray. "Sometimes it's also known as 'Sweetbread'."

Next Murray showed them another type of bread. "This bread is Italian," he said. "It's called Ciabatta."

Murray handed the tray of bread to Miss Twitch.

"These are just a few types of bread children," she said. "Let's get back to class and show the others."

"Bye Uncle Murray!" shouted Dionne and Daniel.

Murray smiled, "See you later kids."

After delivering Bernard's bread to the school, the milk-mobile arrived at Boraq the Butcher's Butcher shop.

Murray brought a tray of French loafs into the butcher shop and two bottles of milk.

Rascal appeared hiding behind a telephone box. "Right, now's my chance," he chuckled. "The milk is mine, its mine. Miow!"

Rascal snuck up to the milk-mobile. He drooled at the sight of the milk. "Lets make it four bottles I think," said the greedy cat.

Rascal grabbed the milk and ran off as fast as his little kitty legs would carry him.

Inside the butcher shop, Boraq was giving Murray a lesson in cutting up oxtail meat because that's what butchers do – cut up meat.

Boraq was holding a chopper. "So you must always make sure to be careful of your fingers," he smiled.

"Thanks for those tips," said Murray. "While I'm here I might as well get some sausages for my dinner too."

Boraq went to the back of the butcher shop and came back with the meat. "These are my finest sausages, and I've thrown in some pork chops on the house!"

"Nice one Boraq!" Murray said. "I've got to go now. I'll see you tomorrow."

With that, Murray left the butcher shop.

Rascal had stopped by the road. He was out of breath from running so fast. "Right," he panted. "Time for some good tasty. Miow!"

Rascal was drinking massive gulps of milk when he saw the milk-mobile coming down the road.

"Oh no," he cried! "That pesky Murray!" He picked up his milk and made a run for it.

As Rascal ran down the road, the milk-mobile was getting closer and closer. "Oh no," he cried!

The milk-mobile caught up to Rascal, and Murray beeped twice. BEEP BEEP!

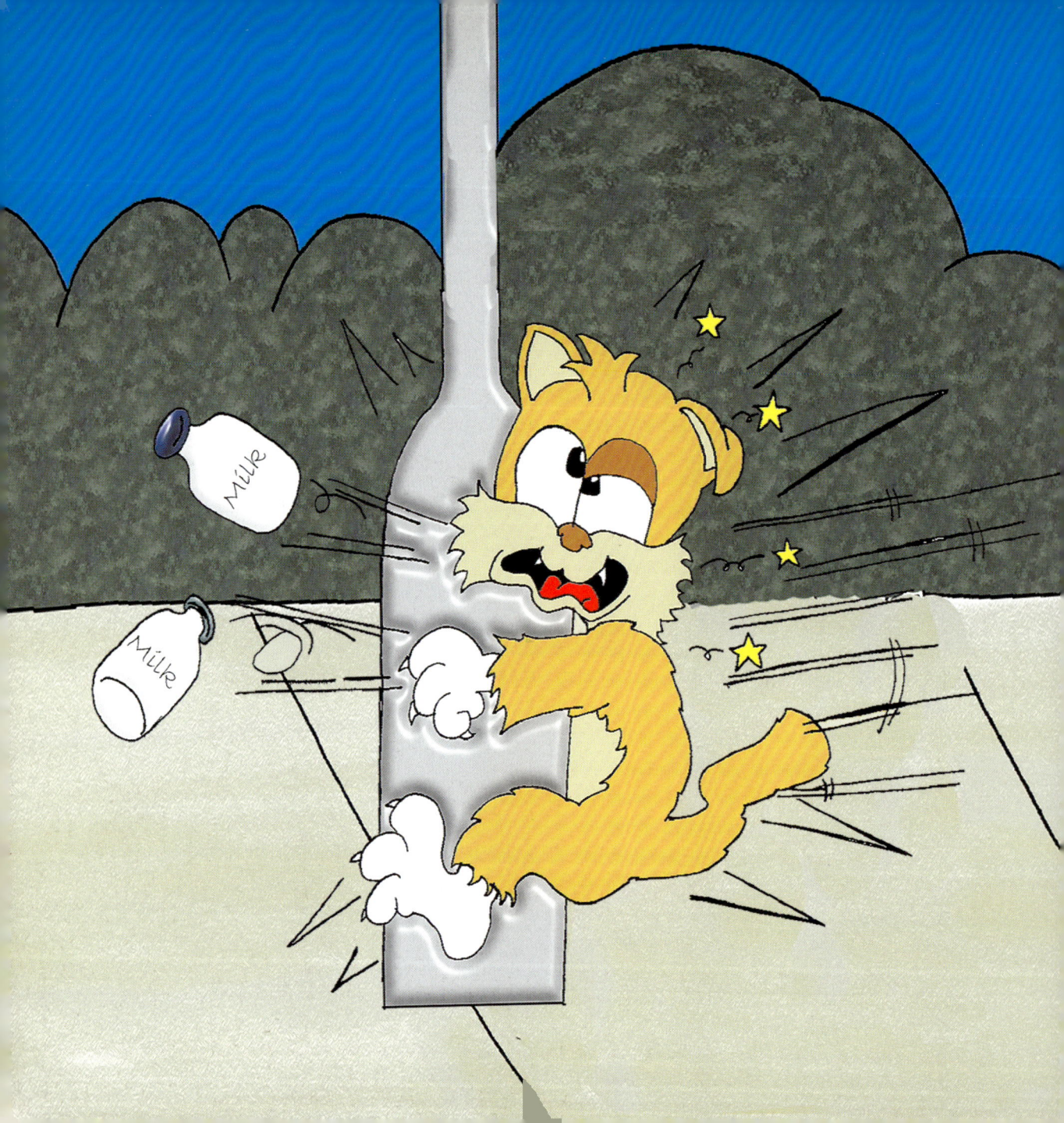

Rascal looked at Murray and smiled. "You can't catch me. Tee hee!" He said.

But he wasn't looking where he was going and went 'SMACK, BANG!' right into a lamppost!

The milk bottles went flying and smashed onto the ground!

Rascal started to cry. "Not again! My delicious milk is gone. I'll get you next time Murray! I'll get you!" Rascal sobbed. "Boo hoo, waaah," he cried, and cried, and cried.

THE END